The Mystery
of the
Pyramids

Written by Max Greenslade

Flying Start
to Literacy®

Contents

Introduction

All around the world, on every continent, there are some amazing structures that were built during ancient times, more than 4500 years ago. Many are still standing and can be visited as tourist attractions. Some are still used today, as they would have been used in ancient times.

The Arles amphitheatre in France was built 2000 years ago and is still used today for bullfights.

Although we know many facts about how most of these buildings were made, some ancient structures in North Africa have intrigued and puzzled people around the world for thousands of years – the pyramids of ancient Egypt. Who built them? How did they do it? And for what purpose?

Scientists and researchers from around the world have studied these monuments to try to explain the mysteries of these amazing structures. But they all have different theories!

Chapter 1
The pyramid makers

There are over 100 pyramids in Egypt, but when people talk about the pyramids of ancient Egypt, they are usually talking about the pyramids of Giza. These huge structures are just outside Egypt's capital Cairo – a sprawling, crowded city of 16 million people, which did not exist when the pyramids were built.

The pyramids of Giza, on the outskirts of Cairo

Each year, more than four million tourists come to gaze at and wonder about these famous, awe-inspiring structures.

When people visit the pyramids, it must be hard to imagine them as they were in ancient Egypt. Today, they are surrounded by souvenir sellers and tour operators. There is even a well-known pizza restaurant opposite the site of the pyramids.

Most people believe that when they were built they were the memorials and final resting places of three mighty rulers of a rich and powerful ancient kingdom. But recently, some people have questioned this because it cannot be proved without a doubt that these pyramids were the final resting places for these kings.

Who were the ancient Egyptians?

Nearly 6000 years ago, along the fertile banks of the Nile River in Northern Africa, farmers raised livestock and grew crops. Over time, they became skilled craftspeople, who created art, jewellery, tools and pottery. They developed mathematics and language systems, as well as religious customs. They built ships, majestic temples and eventually the pyramids.

Gradually, over a period of about 1000 years, they became a powerful civilisation. The ancient Egyptians and their world remained virtually unchanged for 5000 years.

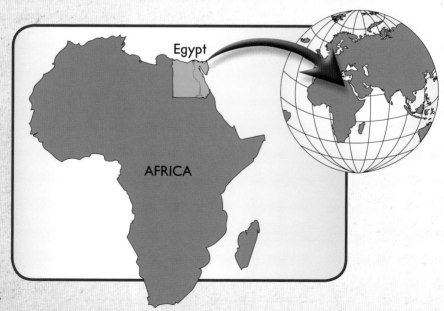

Egypt

AFRICA

The kings

The rulers of Egypt were kings, later called pharaohs. The ancient Egyptians believed that their rulers were gods that had once lived on Earth. Because of this belief, the kings had immense power. They were worshipped as god-kings.

The kings controlled every aspect of Egyptian life. They ruled over all the people that lived on the banks of the Nile River. They owned all the land and everything on it. They made the laws and collected taxes. They also performed religious rituals, which connected ordinary citizens to their gods.

9

Death and the afterlife

Part of the religion of the ancient Egyptians was the belief that when you died, your body travelled into another world called the afterlife. The bodies of kings, queens and other important people were preserved by treating them with oils and wrapping them in cloth. These are commonly called "mummies". They were then put into a decorated coffin called a sarcophagus, which had the likeness of the person painted on the outside.

This picture shows the process of mummification, which was a special way of preparing the body for the afterlife.

An Egyptian mummy inside a sarcophagus

The rulers of ancient Egypt wanted their afterlife to be just as magnificent as their life in Egypt.

To achieve this, they spent much of their lives planning and building their magnificent tombs, so that their bodies would be safe after they were dead. This was why the pyramids were built.

Chapter 2
Pyramid-building frenzy

The first pyramids were built more than 4500 years ago. Building began during the reign of King Sneferu, who ruled for about 30 years. He was the first ruler of ancient Egypt to develop what we know as pyramid-shaped monuments.

The pyramid building continued for about 1000 years. During that time, King Khufu, King Khafre and King Menkaure built the Pyramids of Giza. Then, around 1800 BCE, pyramid building stopped completely. Pyramids were never again built in Egypt.

Pyramid building in ancient Egypt

c. 2670 BCE–2650 BCE	Meidum, Bent and Red Pyramids are constructed during the reign of King Sneferu
c. 2560 BCE	The Great Pyramid is constructed by King Khufu
c. 2530 BCE	Pyramid of Khafre is built at Giza
c. 2510 BCE	Pyramid of Menkaure is built at Giza

The Meidum Pyramid

The first pyramid that King Sneferu built was the Meidum Pyramid. It was constructed close to the banks of the Nile River. It began as a step pyramid, but the sides were too steep and the stones fell off.

The Bent Pyramid

King Sneferu then had a second pyramid built. It started well, but halfway through the construction they changed the angle. No one knows why. Today it is known as the Bent Pyramid.

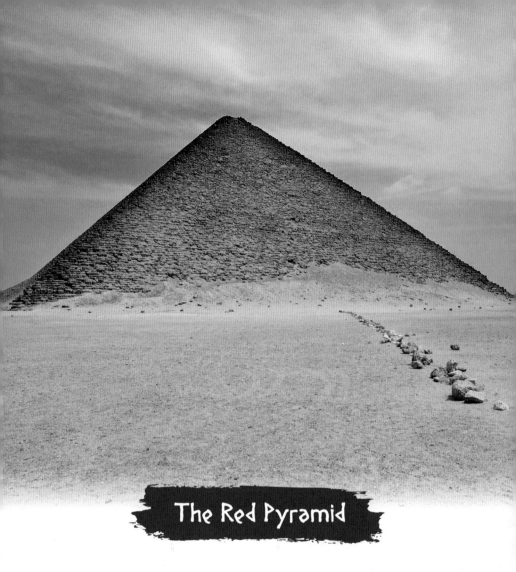

The Red Pyramid

Finally, King Sneferu succeeded with the Red Pyramid. This is the pyramid shape that we know today. He was so satisfied with the Red Pyramid that he decided he would be buried there.

So began the pyramid-building frenzy, which would peak with the building of the magnificent Pyramids of Giza.

The Pyramids of Giza

There are three main pyramids at Giza. The first one was built by Sneferu's son, Khufu, and it is the largest of the three pyramids. It is called the Great Pyramid of Giza and is also known as the Pyramid of Khufu.

The second and third pyramids at Giza were built by Khufu's son and grandson. Each of them are considered to be incredible building achievements.

The three main pyramids at Giza

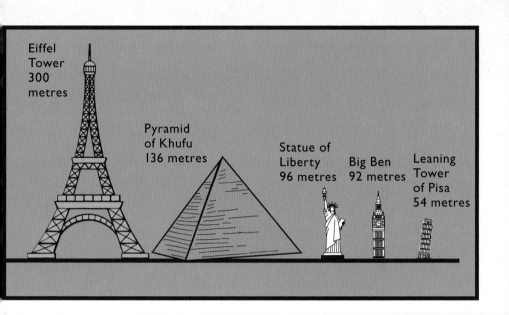

Eiffel Tower 300 metres

Pyramid of Khufu 136 metres

Statue of Liberty 96 metres

Big Ben 92 metres

Leaning Tower of Pisa 54 metres

The Pyramid of Khufu

Chapter 3
How did they build the Great Pyramid of Giza?

The Great Pyramid of Giza took more than 20 years to build and more than two million stones were used to build it. Some of the stones on the pyramid are more than two metres tall and weigh more than seven cars.

So, how did the ancient Egyptians get such huge stones out of the ground and lifted to such a great height? Experts do not agree on how it was done. There are many ideas and theories about how the pyramids were built. As technology becomes more advanced, new evidence may be revealed to prove or disprove long-held ideas.

Theory one

Most archaeologists believe that the ancient Egyptians used simple metal tools to carve huge blocks of stone from quarries near the sites of pyramids. But no tools have been found. They say that the blocks were then pulled and pushed on wooden sleds up ramps. But there is no evidence to show that ramps even existed.

One of the most amazing things about the building of the pyramids was that they were built before the wheel was invented. Everything had to be moved by hand.

Also, no one can explain how these huge blocks of stone were lifted to a height of more than 100 metres. Some experts have suggested that wooden cranes were used. However, this still does not explain how the massive stone blocks could be lifted to such a height.

Theory two

Some experts in concrete and ceramics have tested the pyramid stones and say that many of them are made from a type of cement that looks like stone. They think the ancient Egyptians made wooden moulds in a box shape. They then mixed up the cement and poured it into these moulds. When the cement was dry, the boxes were broken away leaving the blocks of stone.

In this way, the stones could have been made where they were placed on the pyramids. This would mean that the stones did not have to be lifted or carried into place.

Other theories

Recently, some new and radical theories to explain how the pyramids were built have been developed.

One engineer thinks that 90 per cent of the pyramids are made of rubble and covered in an outer layer of limestone.

Another researcher, an architect, came up with the theory that the pyramids were built from the inside out, using a spiral ramp on the inside. He claims that the ramp still exists underneath the outer layer of stones.

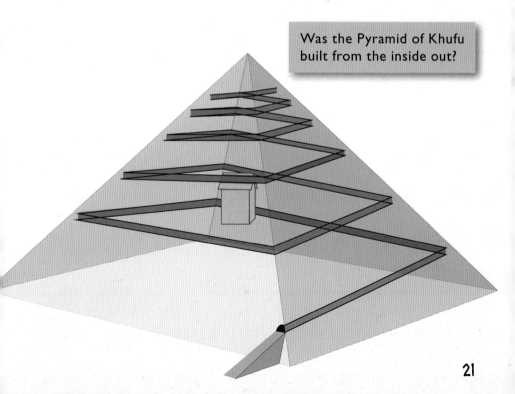

Was the Pyramid of Khufu built from the inside out?

Chapter 4
Who built the pyramids?

The pyramids of Egypt are incredible structures that were built with great precision. Most experts agree that it would have taken thousands of people to design and build the pyramids. But who were the actual builders?

A 19th century image showing how the pyramids might have looked while they were being constructed.

Slaves?

For a long time, most people believed that the ancient Egyptians used slaves to build the pyramids. But at the time that the pyramids were built, there were not that many slaves in Egypt. It was not until much later that slaves lived in Egypt. Historians believe that when ancient Egyptians went to war with other nations they did bring back slaves. But that was after the pyramid-building phase.

So, if slaves didn't build the pyramids, then who did?

This picture is from the ancient Egyptian temple of Abu Simbel and shows Nubian and Ethiopian prisoners.

Paid workers?

Archaeologists have discovered the ruins of houses and bakeries, which they believe would have been used to house and feed the army of builders. And, recently, the ancient graves of Egyptians have been found near the pyramids. Buried in these graves are jars of what was once beer and bread for the afterlife.

Some experts believe that this proves that pyramid workers were respected and paid.

This model of an ancient Egyptian bakery was found in a tomb.

Citizens paying tax?

The "paid worker" theory has been challenged by people who believe that the pyramid workers were citizens working on the pyramids as a form of tax. Instead of paying taxes in food or in other ways, they would have contributed their labour.

Another theory about the workers is that when the Nile River flooded each year and the farmers and peasants could not work on their land, they worked on the pyramids as a way to earn money and to show their love and respect for their king.

Many ideas and theories have been suggested about who built the pyramids and, again, because there is no conclusive proof, no one knows for sure.

Farmers paid taxes to the pharaoh. Some people think they paid their taxes with labour.

Chapter 5
Why did they build the pyramids?

Most archaeologists think that the pyramids were built to house the bodies of rulers after they died, along with food, riches, comforts and even servants who would serve them in the afterlife. But no one knows for sure. This is because no mummies or treasure have ever been found in a pyramid.

This picture shows people inspecting an empty chamber inside the Pyramid of Khufu.

Archaeologists say that there is a simple explanation – that soon after burial, the pyramids were broken into, and everything, including the mummies, was stolen.

Because of the lack of evidence regarding the use of pyramids as a burial site, there are a huge variety of other theories and opinions about their use.

The most famous ancient Egyptian king is Tutankhamen. His tomb, which contained riches and remains, was found under a pile of rubble in 1922. Tutankhamen was buried in an underground chamber in about 1323 BCE. This was long after the ancient Egyptians stopped building pyramids.

Khufu's tomb

Archaeologists are eager to prove that the Pyramid of Khufu was used as a tomb. A chamber in the pyramid contains a stone coffin (sarcophagus), which archaeologists say is evidence that Khufu was buried there.

This is the stone coffin found in a chamber in the Pyramid of Khufu. Is it large enough to hold a mummy?

But others point out that the sarcophagus is neither large enough to hold a mummy nor is it decorated, which seems strange if it held the remains of a god-king.

This is a model of a pyramid with a section cut away to show the chambers and passages.

Most pyramids were built as solid structures, like huge tombstones, with burial chambers under the ground. However, inside Khufu's pyramid there are complex chambers and passageways. More have recently been discovered. Technology is currently being used to scan inside the pyramid to see if there are yet undiscovered passageways and rooms.

It is hoped that the new technology will reveal hidden chambers where they will one day discover a tomb and perhaps the buried treasures of the great king.

A rover robot is sent into an air shaft in the Pyramid of Khufu to discover information about what is inside

Conclusion

There are so many theories about who built the pyramids in Egypt, as well as how and why they were built. As long as the pyramids are still standing, there will never be a shortage of experts coming forward with the "truth" about the pyramids.

But this is what makes the pyramids so fascinating. It brings the history of their creation alive and it gives people a connection to the ancient past.

The Pyramid of Khufu (second from the right) is one of the seven wonders of the ancient world and is the only one of the wonders that still exists today.

The pyramids make people wonder about a civilisation that was perhaps so advanced that they had skills and ancient technology that we cannot recreate today. Were the skills and technology lost when their civilisation disappeared?

Perhaps we will never know the truth about the pyramids, and they will always remain a mystery.

Glossary

ceramics the art of making objects out of clay

civilisation a well-organised society that shares laws, customs and ways of life

labour people's ability to do work

mummy a dead body treated with oils and wrapped in strips of cloth before burial

radical theories a theory is a way of understanding or explaining a fact or an event; a radical theory is a new and very different explanation than traditional explanations.

religious ritual a formal ceremony that was practised as part of a religion

sarcophagus a stone coffin from ancient times

tax a proportion of a person's income that is paid to the government